## To the Reader . . .

"World Cities" focuses on cities as a way to learn about the major civilizations of the world. Each civilization has at its roots the life of one or more cities. Learning about life in the great cities is essential to understanding the past and present of the world and its people.

People live in cities for many reasons. For one thing, they value what cities can offer them culturally. Culture thrives in all cities. It is expressed in visual arts, music, and ethnic celebrations. In fact, a city's greatness is often measured by the richness of culture that it offers those who live there.

Many people choose to live in cities for economic reasons. Cities offer a variety of jobs and other economic opportunities. Many city dwellers have found prosperity through trade. Nearly all the world's great cities were founded on trade—the voluntary exchange of goods and services between people. The great cities remain major economic centers.

City living can, of course, have its disadvantages. Despite these disadvantages, cities continue to thrive. By reading about the people, culture, geography, and economy of various metropolitan centers, you will understand why. You will also understand why the world is becoming more and more urban. Finally, you will learn what it is that makes each world city unique.

Mark Schug, Consulting Editor
Co-author of *Teaching Social Studies in the
Elementary School* and *Community Study*

## CONSULTING EDITOR

Mark C. Schug
Professor of Curriculum and Instruction
University of Wisconsin-Milwaukee

## EDITORIAL

Amy Bauman, Project Editor
Barbara J. Behm
Judith Smart, Editor-in-Chief

## ART/PRODUCTION

Suzanne Beck, Art Director
Carole Kramer, Designer
Thom Pharmakis, Photo Researcher
Eileen Rickey, Typesetter
Andrew Rupniewski, Production Manager

Reviewed for accuracy by:
Jerry Johnson
Professor of Economics and
    Director of Center for Economic Education
University of Wisconsin-Eau Claire

James H. Terada, Ph.D.
Professor of Management and
    Executive Director of International Activities
Front Range Community College, Westminster, Colorado

Haiku on page 36 reprinted from *Japan: The Land and Its People* by Sophy Hoare. © Macdonald Children's Books, 1975, 1986. Photographs on pages 9, 10, 14, 16, 18, 19, 26, 38, 40, 41, 50, 51, 57, 58 through courtesy of the International Society for Educational Information, Inc.

Library of Congress Number: 89-10431

1 2 3 4 5 6 7 8 9          93 92 91 90 89

**Library of Congress Cataloging in Publication Data**

Davis, Jim, 1940-
  Tokyo.
  (World cities)

  Summary: Explores the history, cultural heritage, demographics, geography, and economic and natural resources of Tokyo.
  1. Tokyo (Japan)—Juvenile literature. [1. Tokyo (Japan)] I. Hawke, Sharryl Davis. II. Title. III. Series: Davis, Jim, 1940-  . World cities.
DS896.35.D37  1989  915.2'135     [B] [92]     89-10431
ISBN 0-8172-3032-7 (lib bdg.)

**Cover Photo: Click / Chicago © Tony Stone Worldwide**

# WORLD CITIES

# CITIES

# TOKYO

## JAMES E. DAVIS
## AND
## SHARRYL DAVIS HAWKE

RAINTREE PUBLISHERS
Milwaukee

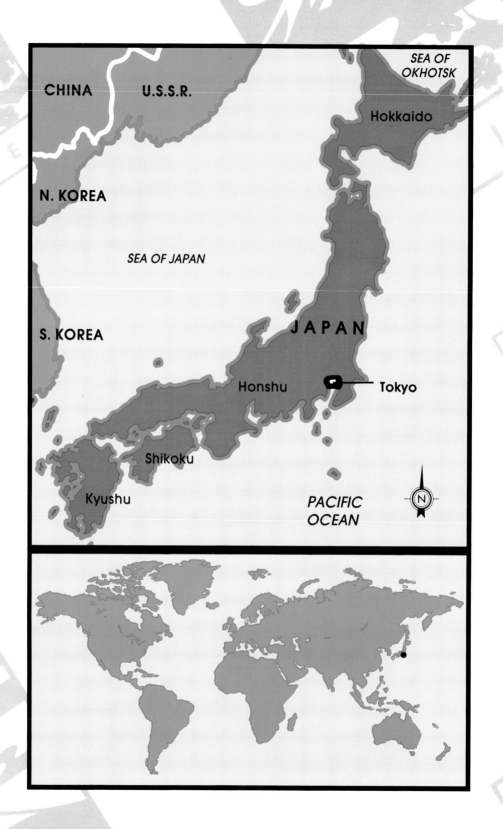

# Contents

# Introduction

Tokyo is the capital of Japan, which the Japanese call *Nippon,* "the Land of the Rising Sun." Eleven million people live in the city. Tokyo features tall, modern buildings, fast commuter trains, streets teeming with people and crowded with automobiles, and colorful signs calling attention to McDonald's restaurants and Coca-Cola. It is also an ancient city where traditions and customs still play important roles, as a glance at a Japanese home and Japanese schools will show.

## A Japanese Home

Most homes in Tokyo, as in other Japanese cities, are small because building space is limited. As is custom, people remove their shoes upon entering a Japanese home. Instead of rugs or carpeting, *tatami* mats, which are made of straw, cover the floors. Paper screens fastened to wooden frames are often used to divide rooms. Similar sliding screens open to the outside and to a small garden if there is space for one.

When eating or relaxing, people usually sit on cushions on the floor instead of on chairs. In public, the Japanese usually wear American- or European-style clothing. At home though, men, women, and children relax in *kimonos,* comfortable silk robes that tie at the waist. At night, thick quilts called *futons* are unrolled and placed on the tatami mats to serve as beds.

Most homes have an *o-furo,* a Japanese bath, which is a wooden tub of

*Traditional houses are built with frail walls of paper and wood. Where there is space enough, a garden will surround the house.*

*Rice, fish, and vegetables are the ingredients of this traditional Japanese meal.*

water heated by gas. People scrub, clean, and rinse themselves before entering the tub for a relaxing soak. In the past, there were large public baths, where people met and talked with their friends in the o-furos. Some public baths remain today.

The traditional Japanese evening meal includes rice, fish, and vegetables. The Japanese eat fish prepared in many different ways, but a very popular way is to eat it raw. Raw fish is called *sashimi*, and rice with raw fish on top is called *sushi*. The Japanese also enjoy beef and vegetables in a soy sauce, which is called *sukiyaki*, and

shrimp or vegetables fried in a light batter, called *tempura*.

## School Days

Beginning at age six, young Japanese spend 5½ days a week, 230 days a year, in school. New classes begin on April 1 and continue through March of the following year. There are some school holidays, and a vacation time each year from late in July through August.

On their way to school, students often wear yellow hats and carry yellow book bags so they can easily be seen by motorists. When they cross a street, they pick up yellow flags kept in a bucket at the curb. They wave the flags to stop traffic as they cross. When reaching the other side, students place the flags in another bucket for the return.

In school, students sit at desks facing a chalkboard. They study mathematics, science, social studies, music, and art, and they have physical education classes. Students also learn the grammar of their language and how to write it.

Japanese is written in characters called *kanji*. There are thousands of

*Opposite: Japanese schoolchildren wear yellow caps to make themselves more visible to drivers (above). In the classroom, students learn practical skills, such as sewing (below).*

*Students learn to print calligraphy with brushes and ink (above). The kanji characters representing the first ten numbers are shown (below).*

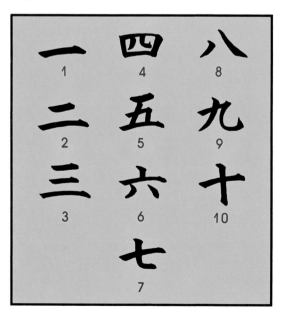

kanji, and each one has meaning. Students learn about two thousand of them in school. Japanese also has symbols that stand for sounds. There are ninety-six of these symbols, which are called *kana*. Kana and kanji are used together in Japanese writing.

Instead of handwriting, Japanese students practice calligraphy, which is a form of writing that looks like careful little drawings. They learn to make these characters with a brush. And when the Japanese read and write, they go in columns from the top of the page to the bottom, from right to left, and from what seems like the back of a book to the front. In Japan, 99 percent of the people can read and write. This is the highest rate of any country in the world.

Japanese young people are not required to go to high school, although nearly all of them do. After high school graduation, many go on to a college, a university, or a technical school. Tokyo has more than one hundred four-year colleges and universities. Hihon University is the largest. It holds eighty thousand students.

## An Island Nation

Tokyo is located on the southern shore of the island of Honshu, one of the four main islands of Japan. The others are Hokkaido, Shikoku, and Kyushu. On a globe, you will find Japan just off the coast of South Korea in the Pacific Ocean. If you wish, by using a piece of string and the globe's scale of miles, you can get an idea of how far Japan is from where you live.

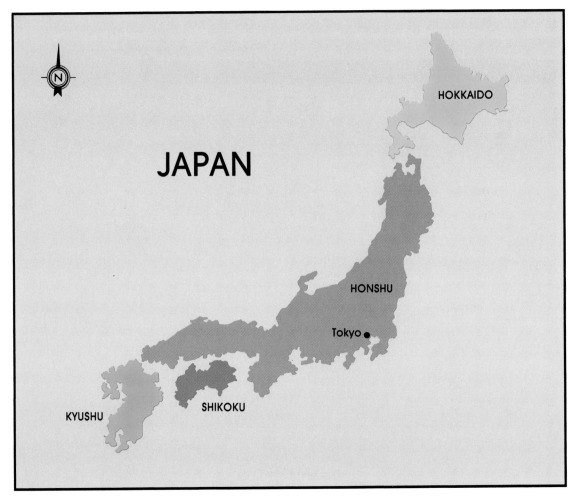

Altogether, Japan is smaller than the state of California. It is a beautiful country of mountains and a few plains, surrounded by sea.

Tokyo is situated in an open area called the Kanto Plain, along Tokyo Bay. Several rivers flow into the bay, including the Sumida, Arakawa, Edogawa, and the Tama. The part of Tokyo closest to the bay is called Shitamachi. This low plain area was once used for rice paddies and farming. Houses and factories now cover the land.

The part of Tokyo just next to Shitamachi is called the Musashino Plateau. It was formed by ash from volcanic eruptions thousands of years ago. The soil is reddish. Homes, schools, hospitals, and parks now cover this area. In the southern part of the plateau, the Tama River winds through hills and mountains. Along the slopes of these hills, Japanese tend mulberry and tea fields. There are also beautiful parks here, and it is a favorite spot for picnicking and hiking.

*The Imperial Palace occupies the center of Tokyo. Rebuilt since World War II, the palace is surrounded by moats and gardens dating from the 1400s.*

Although the most recent major quake was in 1923 at Tokyo, Japan remains a land of earthquakes. Earthquakes and the great fires that often followed them have destroyed many buildings and killed many people throughout Japanese history.

Japan is also vulnerable to typhoons —storms that are something like hurricanes and cyclones combined. The low plains of Japan are in danger of being flooded during typhoons, and the Japanese have built large dikes near Tokyo Bay to help prevent that.

Tokyo's rainy season is in June and July. These months are followed by a hot summer, a colorful fall, and a mild winter with little snow. The history of Tokyo is the story of how a small fishing and farming village on a small island grew to become one of the most important cities in the world.

*The Great Kanto Earthquake of 1923 destroyed large sections of Tokyo. Sixty thousand people lost their lives in the quake and the fires which followed.*

Kyodo News Service

WORLD

CITIES

# How Tokyo Began

A Japanese legend tells the story of how two gods who were brother and sister formed the Japanese islands. According to this story, these gods dipped a magnificent sword made of jewels into the sea. As they brought it back out of the water and lifted it to the heavens, drops of water fell off the sword and into the sea. These drops formed the islands of Japan.

## The First Japanese

Chinese records dating to A.D. 300 refer to the Japanese as the "polite and virtuous people of Wa." Many people were living in Japan long before that, however.

No one really knows where the first Japanese, called the Jomon people, came from or when they reached the islands. They could have come from Asia or from the north or the south. The Jomon people lived in various settlements in Japan, fishing and gathering nuts and berries. The largest number of them probably lived just north of Tokyo. Some Jomon artifacts that have been found here are estimated to be more than ten thousand years old.

Sometime before 300 B.C., the Yayoi people came to Japan from Korea. They introduced farming and metalworking to the Jomon people. For the next six hundred years, more and more people came to Japan from the Asian mainland.

Different tribes were scattered throughout the Japanese countryside,

15

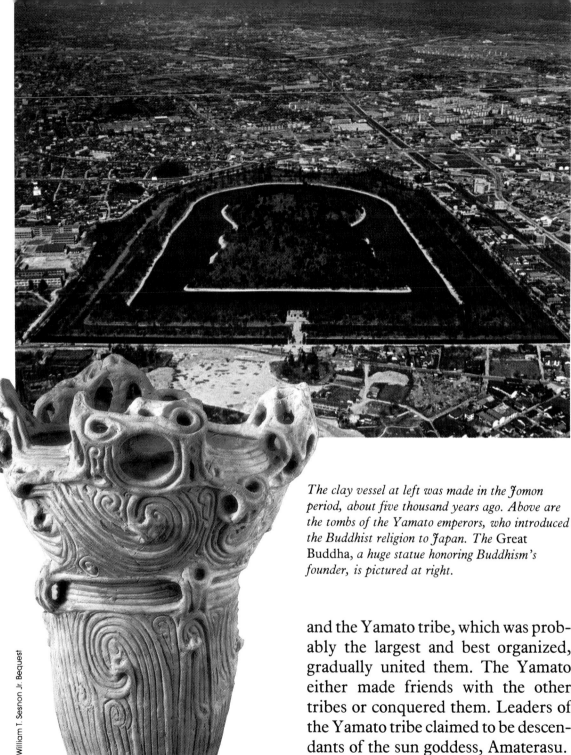

*The clay vessel at left was made in the Jomon period, about five thousand years ago. Above are the tombs of the Yamato emperors, who introduced the Buddhist religion to Japan. The* Great Buddha, *a huge statue honoring Buddhism's founder, is pictured at right.*

and the Yamato tribe, which was probably the largest and best organized, gradually united them. The Yamato either made friends with the other tribes or conquered them. Leaders of the Yamato tribe claimed to be descendants of the sun goddess, Amaterasu.

In the fifth century, a Yamato leader took the title of *emperor,* which means

ruler of an empire. The title is usually passed down from generation to generation in the same family. It was soon after this that Buddhism, which began in India in the sixth century B.C., came to Japan by way of China. Buddhism is the religion of much of central and eastern Asia and is based on the teachings of a man named Siddhārtha Gautama, who became Buddha.

## When Tokyo Was Edo

Until the twelfth century, the place where Tokyo is today was a marshy, wooded area. A warrior family said to have the name Edo lived there, and Edo became the name of the city. It was later renamed Tokyo.

Japanese records say that the capital moved each time an emperor died. For a time in the 700s, Nara was the capital. Located in central Japan, Nara was modeled after the large and beautiful cities of China. In 790, Kyoto became the capital, and once that occurred, the emperor lived there until 1868.

Even though there was a central government, many individual and independent families had large estates that became communities in these early days. The families managed these communities themselves.

In 1192, a warrior named Minamoto Yoritomo took power away from the emperor and set up a military government, called the *shogunate,* to rule the nation. Minamoto Yoritomo was the first *shogun. Daimyos* were lords who ruled the different regions of Japan for the shogun. *Samurai* were the famous warriors who served the daimyos.

Yoritomo set up his headquarters at Kamakura, south of Edo, and until the nineteenth century there were two centers of government: the shogun

Jingo-ji

*Minamoto Yoritomo became Japan's first shogun, or military ruler, in 1192. The shoguns controlled Japan until 1868.*

and the emperor. The real power lay with the shogun. The emperor in Kyoto had little authority.

In 1274, Kublai Khan, leader of the Mongols of central Asia, sent his men to invade Japan. Kublai Khan's armies had overrun many countries in Asia, but in Japan, they failed because of stormy weather. In 1281, Kublai Khan again sent his men to invade Japan, but again the weather stopped them. This time it was a typhoon, which destroyed the ships and killed most of the Mongols. In Japanese history this typhoon is known as *kamikaze,* or "divine wind." The Japanese people say it was sent by the gods to protect them.

In the 1400s, a warrior named Ota Dokan served the daimyo who ruled the region that included Edo. To protect his region, Ota Dokan built a fortress in Edo. This fortress, known as Edo Castle, changed the small village of Edo into an important military city.

In 1542, a ship from Portugal, carrying goods to trade, arrived in Japan. The Portuguese traders on this ship became the first Europeans to enter Japan. The Japanese welcomed the traders, just as they welcomed the missionaries who came later to teach the Christian religion. Over the next one hundred years, some 300,000 Japanese became Christians.

Despite this encouraging reception, not all Japanese people were eager to

*During the late 1200s, Mongols twice tried invading Japan. Both times, storms at sea kept the Mongols from landing their ships.*

Imperial Household Agency

19

see the foreigners in their country. Some people were concerned that the outsiders wanted to rule Japan. But by the late 1500s, Japan's military government was growing stronger, and the country was more united. Still, power struggles were common. In 1590, a great daimyo named Tokugawa Ieyasu took possession of Edo Castle and set up his military headquarters there. In 1603, following a struggle for power, Ieyasu became the new shogun. Edo was suddenly the capital of Japan.

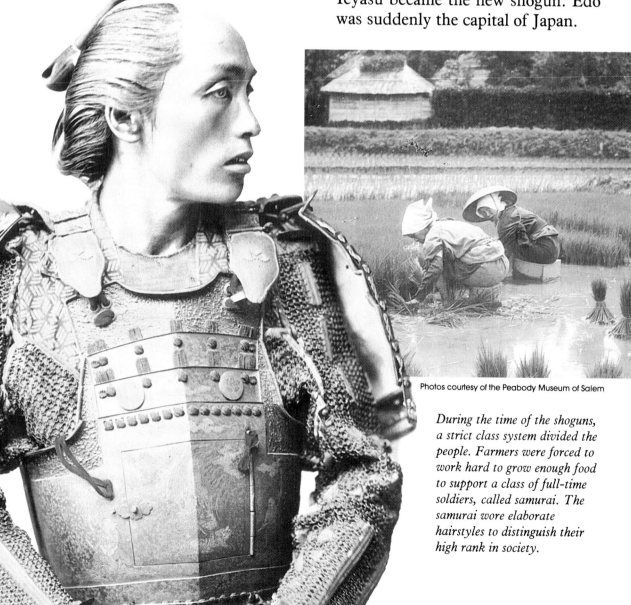

Photos courtesy of the Peabody Museum of Salem

*During the time of the shoguns, a strict class system divided the people. Farmers were forced to work hard to grow enough food to support a class of full-time soldiers, called samurai. The samurai wore elaborate hairstyles to distinguish their high rank in society.*

# Tokugawa Ieyasu Changes Edo and Japan

Once Ieyasu became shogun, he took complete control of Japan. The Tokugawa family held power over all the largest cities, mines, ports, and large personal estates. The shogun himself controlled most of the rice that was grown, and rice was Japan's most important crop. The Tokugawa family ruled this way for more than 250 years. During that time, the little fishing village of Edo grew from a village of several hundred thatched huts into a magnificent city. As the population swelled, Ieyasu helped the city keep pace. Because much of Edo was a marshy area, the shogun organized great projects to fill in the land, construct canals, and build a truly great city.

Ieyasu also established an order of social standing, or hierarchy. At the top were the nobles—the shogun, his daimyos, and their families. Next came the famous samurai warriors, followed by the farmers. Below this level came the crafts people and finally the merchants. Policemen enforced the shogun's strict control. They spied on people to make sure that they were following orders and carrying out their jobs. To keep control of the distant regions, Ieyasu ruled that all the daimyos must attend court at Edo every other year. He also decreed that their

*The growth of Edo during the 1600s created a new class of merchants and peddlers, who sold goods to the noble families living at the shogun's court.*

families must live in Edo permanently. Merchants, crafts people, and artists flocked to the city to provide for the needs of the nobles and their families.

As Edo and Japan grew, Ieyasu began to worry more and more about the influence of the foreigners. He and other Japanese leaders began to suspect that the missionaries' activities, along with those of traders, might lead to the conquest of Japan by Portugal or some other European nation. In 1612, Hidetada, who became shogun after Ieyasu, ordered all missionary activity in Japan to cease. The people of Japan were not allowed to travel abroad, and foreigners—especially Europeans—were not allowed to visit Japan. No large ships for ocean travel could be built. Japan became a closed society. It would remain so until the middle of the nineteenth century.

## Edo in the 1600s and 1700s

The 1600s and 1700s were a time of prosperity and growth for Edo. It was during these years that weaving and pottery became important industries, and beautiful silk cloth became an especially important product. These small industries provided a strong base for the economy. Although the merchants may have held a low social status, they accumulated much wealth during this time.

In 1657, almost half the city was destroyed by fire, but the people of Edo worked together to quickly rebuild. Under the rule of Ieyasu and his successors, Edo became not only the political center of the country but the center for trade and art as well. The population grew to more than one million people by the early 1700s. Edo was probably the largest city in the world at that time.

In 1707, Mount Fuji erupted. The mountain is 40 miles (64 km) from Edo, so the city was not damaged, but ash from the eruption fell on the city like black snow, covering everything.

*By the 1700s, the city had become well known for the beautiful silks produced there. In this nineteenth-century photo, spinners work the silk fibers into the strong thread used to weave these fabrics.*

# Tokyo in the Nineteenth and Twentieth Centuries

During the first part of the nineteenth century, life in Edo continued as usual. However, change was just over the horizon, in the form of four warships from the United States.

America and some European nations wished to establish trade with Japan. The Japanese government turned down every request, however. Japan was not interested in opening its ports—and its country—to foreigners.

Then in 1853, the American government sent four ships to Japan under Commodore Matthew C. Perry to demand trade with Japan. The shogun felt that Japan was not strong enough to resist the request for trade. He asked the emperor and the top daimyos for advice. They told him to force the Americans to leave. However, because Japan's defenses were so weak, the shogun gave in to Commodore Perry's demand. In 1854, the government signed an agreement to set up limited trade between Japan and America. The treaty opened two ports to the Americans: Hakodate and Shimoda. Soon, Great Britain, the Netherlands, and Russia gained the right to trade with Japan, too.

The emperor's court was against the shogun's decision. Members of the court, along with some of the powerful daimyos, staged revolts against the shogun. In 1868, they declared that the authority of the emperor would be restored. Eventually, the Tokugawa shogun gave up his power.

## Edo Becomes Tokyo

The Emperor Meiji who came to power at this time was still a boy. His advisors moved the capital from Kyoto, in western Japan, to Edo. Edo was then renamed Tokyo, meaning "eastern capital." As the new ruler grew up and his court established its power over the country, the role of the samurai disappeared.

The warrior caste lost its high social standing. In 1876, former samurai were ordered not to wear their swords

*The Emperor Meiji led Japan into the modern age. He was the first emperor to actually run Japan since the 1100s.*

any more. With this order, they lost their most important symbol of prestige. Samurai and their familes left the capital. Soon, many of the merchants and crafts people who had taken care of their needs left, too. Tokyo lost about half its population. But as trade developed and as American and European machinery and other technology were introduced, the city soon came to life again and grew rapidly.

It is true that the Emperor Meiji's court came to power by opposing trade agreements with the Western world. But the court soon found it difficult to resist the Western powers. They decided to meet the challenge with the slogan "rich country, strong military."

## Learning New Ways

Instead of letting others control them, the Japanese decided to learn as much as they could from foreigners. This knowledge, the Japanese leaders knew, could be used for their own benefit. For the next twenty years, the people of Tokyo and the rest of Japan worked to do this. Experts in a variety of fields were brought in from America and Europe to teach Western methods. In addition, Japanese students were sent abroad to learn about Western industries and ways of making products. They then came back to share the information. The Japanese

*Japanese nobles gather for the proclaiming of the 1889 constitution. Many wore the traditional dress of the samurai. Years earlier, the samurai had been ordered not to wear their swords or armor in public. For formal occasions such as this, many still did.*

adapted what they learned to make it their own.

In 1889, Japan's first constitution, the Meiji Constitution, went into effect. It called for an elected parliament with a prime minister. The emperor was left with little power. The people, however, would accord him deep respect and loyalty, and look upon him almost as a god. The Japanese plan for government seemed like a democracy on the surface, but elder statesmen really were the ones in control.

As Japan's leaders worked to change seemingly unfair trade treaties with other countries, Japan's military power grew. Japan went to war with China in 1895 and with Russia in 1904-1905.

*The bombing of Tokyo during World War II leveled whole sections of the city. After the war, many parts of the city—including the Imperial Palace—were rebuilt from the ground up.*

The British helped Japan in the war with Russia. Japan won both of these wars.

However, the early 1900s were generally difficult years for Japan. Between changes within the country itself, changes in its foreign policy, and World War I (1914-1918), nothing stayed the same for long. In the middle of all the confusion, Tokyo was hit by a terrible earthquake in 1923. More than sixty thousand people lost their lives, and many homes were destroyed by the fires that followed. More than half the people in the city were left homeless. All the major buildings were lost. But the hardworking people of Tokyo rebuilt the city in less than eight years.

## Tokyo During World War II

In the 1930s, Japan set out to conquer China and other lands in Asia. The United States opposed Japan's plans, leading the Japanese to attack Pearl Harbor in Hawaii on December 7, 1941.

The resulting war turned out badly for Japan. The United States bombing raids on Tokyo in 1944 and 1945 were very destructive. About 800,000 buildings were destroyed and more than 250,000 people were reported missing or dead. Many families fled to the countryside during the war. Again, the population of Tokyo was cut in half.

Japan surrendered in September 1945 after the United States dropped an atomic bomb on two of its cities, Hiroshima and Nagasaki. For the first time in the history of Japan, a foreign army was in charge. General Douglas MacArthur commanded the American military forces that occupied Japan until 1952.

Japan had to give up its possessions overseas, and all Japanese soldiers and citizens who had been living in overseas territories had to return home. Out-of-date laws were thrown out, and in 1946, a new constitution was written. Under this constitution, a true parliamentary democracy was set up. The emperor was no longer considered an almost divine person. He would remain only as a symbol to unify the Japanese people.

*On September 2, 1945, Japanese officials surrendered to General Douglas MacArthur. The surrender was signed on board the American battleship U.S.S. Missouri. Japan remained under United States control until 1951.*

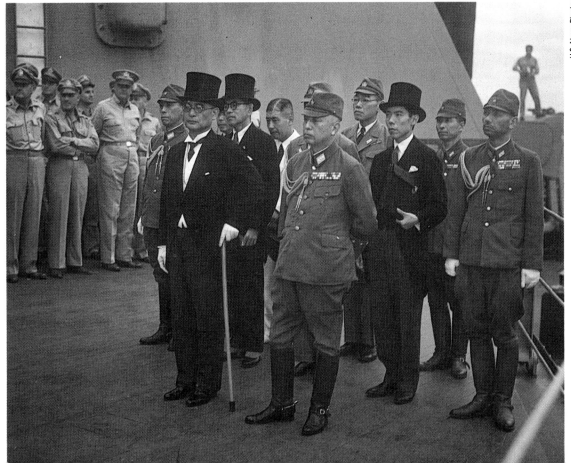

The new parliamentary system created an elected House of Representatives, called a Diet, and a prime minister. A system of courts was established, and the rights of individuals were to be recognized. A system of taxes helped spread the country's wealth. Large industries were broken up into smaller companies.

## Rebuilding Business and Industry

After the war, many Japanese left the countryside to live in cities. The population of Tokyo and other urban areas increased. Many of these people, however, did not have jobs, and they were poor. The most important thing for Tokyo and for all of Japan was to put people back to work and to build a strong economy. The government helped and encouraged industry and trade.

Trade began again with such traditional products as cloth and paper items. At the same time, Japan imported modern machines and other technology from America and Europe.

*Since the war, Tokyo has become one of the most modern-looking cities in the world.*

As industries grew, Japan was soon exporting aircraft, automobiles, motorcycles, and electronic equipment. Japan's steel industry became strong and competitive. Its shipbuilding industry became one of the biggest in the world.

At this time, the government helped industries and businesses more than it did individual people or families. People were encouraged to save and plan ahead to help themselves. Business profits were put back into the companies to increase production.

After World War II, Tokyo grew steadily. It was like a magnet. People were drawn to Tokyo from all over Japan in search of better jobs and better lives. Tokyo was the hub of business, trade, and education. By the 1960s, the population grew so fast that

Nissan Motor Co. Ltd.

Jack Com

the city struggled to supply everyone with housing, food, and water. In spite of the population stress on the city, Tokyo's economy continued to expand.

Automobiles became a top Japanese export. Japan has one car for every five people, but in the United States many families have two or three cars. People in the United States wanted small, reliable, and economical cars at reasonable prices. The Japanese automobile industry was able to produce them, and the American people were ready to buy. The number of Toyotas, Nissans, Hondas, and Mitsubishis in America today shows how successful the Japanese auto industry has been. The electronics industry also has been successful in Japan. Companies such as Sony export stereos, television sets, and videocassette recorders.

Japan has become so successful in international trade that many countries have grown concerned about competing with the Japanese. Japan produces and exports many high-quality goods. It is now one of the most successful countries in the world. In the 1980s, other countries looked to

*Japanese grasp of new technologies has made the country a manufacturing giant (above left). Tokyo's growing population has caused overcrowding in the city's older sections. New apartments are built to provide more living space (left).*

Japan Information Center

JNTO

*Emperor Akihito is a trained biologist who has published more than twenty-four papers on Pacific Ocean fish. At right is a footbridge on the grounds of the emperor's palace.*

the Japanese for ways to improve their economies.

At the end of the 1980s, the people of Tokyo and all Japan again experienced a great change. In January 1989, Emperor Hirohito died at the age of eighty-seven. Hirohito had been emperor for sixty-two years. He had guided the country through the difficult post-war time. Upon his death, his son, Akihito, became the new emperor.

WORLD

CITIES

# More Customs and Traditions

Tokyo has been rebuilt since the end of World War II. It is now much more of a modern city. Its buildings look like many found in the United States and Europe. The people of Tokyo wear American- and European- style clothing. They have taken to such fast-foods as McDonald's hamburgers and Kentucky Fried Chicken.

Japan's history tells much about Japanese customs. Remember, Japan is an island nation, one that remained apart from much of the world for a long time. During this time, the Japanese people developed customs of their own. They also developed Japanese versions of customs and beliefs that came from nearby countries such as China and Korea.

## Counting and Calendars

Part of the Japanese writing system is based on the Chinese. The counting system uses both Chinese words and Japanese words, and there are different ways to count different types of objects. For instance, flat things are counted by adding *mai* to the end of the number. Long cylindrical objects have the ending *hon* at the end of the number. Pets, such as cats and dogs, have the ending *hiki* (head) after the number.

Today, when Japanese businesspeople write letters to people in other countries, they use the same calendar used in Europe and the United States, which was introduced to Japan in 1872. But the Japanese keep track of the years in other ways too. One is by using the first year of an emperor's reign as a reference point. For example, the Meiji era began in 1867, so 1870 would be called "Fourth Year of Meiji."

The Japanese also keep track of dates on an ancient Chinese zodiac calendar. This calendar is divided into years that are named for the twelve animals associated with Buddha. For example, one year is the year of the rabbit and another the year of the dragon. The cycle repeats every twelve years.

## Japanese Religions

Many Japanese customs come from religious traditions. There are two major religions in Japan: Shinto and Buddhism. Both are concerned with different aspects of living and they easily exist side by side. Many Japanese consider themselves members of both religions.

The Shinto religion, whose name means the "way of the gods," began in Japan. Shintoists honor nature and believe that humans should live in harmony with the sun, mountains, trees, animals, and other parts of nature. The gods of nature are called *kami*. In Shinto, there are festivals that celebrate harmony with the kami or help recreate it. These festivals occur throughout the year.

The most special kami are worshiped at shrines. A *torii* is a tall, wooden arch or gateway that marks the entrance to a shrine. *Torii* means "bird perch," and the gate is shaped like a rooster's perch. It is said that when time began, the rooster crowed. This woke up the sun goddess, who brought light to the world. Kami shrines often are surrounded by beautiful gardens to represent a bond with nature.

Buddhism was introduced to Japan from China in A.D. 538. At first the Japanese did not accept this religion

*Wooden archways called torii are used to mark the entrances to Shinto temples.*

Harold Pfeiffer

Harold Pfeiffer

Harold Pfeiffer

*New Year's Day is the biggest of Japan's annual festivals. At a Shinto temple, incense is burned for figures representing ancestors (above). A banner celebrates the Buddhist year of the rabbit (left). Slips of paper printed with horoscopes are tied to a temple fence (opposite).*

because it was foreign. Soon, however, it caught on and even became fashionable. The Shinto religion centers mostly around nature and natural events, while Buddhism centers around the mind and spirit. In this way, the two religions work well together.

Once Buddhism was accepted in Japan, it began taking on different Japanese forms. One of the best-known forms of Japanese Buddhism is *Zen*. Followers of Zen practice meditation and self-discipline to develop the mind and the spirit.

## Japanese Festivals

Festivals are celebrated throughout the year in Tokyo. Some have their beginnings in Shinto and some in Buddhism. There are festivals for New Year's Day, for Buddha's birthday, and for the emperor's birthday, as well as a girls' festival, and a boys' festival, to mention just a few. These festivals, called *matsuri,* often include colorful parades, fairs, and special activities and games.

The biggest celebration of the year is New Year's Day, called *Gantan.* All the people dress in kimonos and decorate their homes with branches of pine, bamboo, and plum for good luck. Bells are rung in the Buddhist temples, and Buddhist scriptures are read while people sip *sake,* a wine

Harold Pfeiffer

Campion Photograph

*Contact with nature is important to the Japanese. Even the smallest backyards are planted with greenery.*

A deep love of nature is important in Japanese art, and Zen Buddhism and Shinto influenced many of the art forms. Landscape painting, poetry, gardening, and architecture all reflect nature, simplicity, and harmony.

A poem by the famous Japanese poet of the seventeenth century, Basho, shows these qualities. Translated into English it says:

> A crow is perched
> Upon a leafless withered bough—
> The autumn dusk.

This type of poem is called a *haiku.* A haiku captures a moment in time and usually deals with nature. Most haiku are three lines long. Some haiku poets follow formal rules. For instance, they put five syllables in the first line, seven in the second line, and five again in the third line. In ancient Japan, people would gather at parties at the emperor's court to write poetry together. Poetry was a natural part of everyone's life. Friends wrote poems to give to each other as gifts, writing them in calligraphy on beautiful colored paper. Even the samurai wrote poetry.

Many of the temples in Japan are excellent examples of early Buddhist architecture. They have steep, sloping roofs and are usually made of wood with many beautifully carved areas. The *pagoda* is a special type of temple that came from China. It is a tower with a series of upturned roofs.

made from rice. On New Year's Day, people visit their employers, students visit their teachers, and families play special games.

On January 2, children participate in the formal First Writing of the year. They gather to write proverbs, or short sayings, in their finest calligraphy and take them home as decorations.

## Japanese Art

Many of Japan's art forms originally came from China hundreds of years ago. But over the years, they have changed. They have become unique Japanese art forms.

*Chinese culture greatly influenced Japan. From China, the Japanese imported the Buddhist religion and a Buddhist style of temple architecture. The pagoda, shown here, is a type of temple that has a steeply sloped roof and elaborate decorations.*

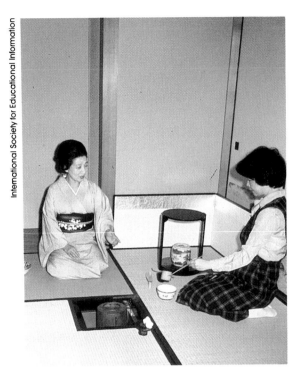

*Students are taught to perform the tea ceremony. Buddhists believe religious truths can be learned from simple tasks.*

A special Japanese ceremony, *sa-do*, was also introduced from China. The sa-do is a tea ceremony, the meaning of which comes from Buddhism. It is said to help the inner character of things show outwardly. Every step of the ceremony and every movement is significant, even the way one drinks the tea.

*Ikebana* is the tradition of flower arranging. This form of art began in the eighth century at the Imperial Court. In Ikebana, the placement of flowers is supposed to show a god at the top, the earth at the foot, and humans in between.

# The Japanese Sense of Belonging

The Japanese have a strong sense of belonging. They belong to the family of their birth, and later to the family into which they marry. Many couples today live apart from their parents, but they still have a sense of responsibility and belonging to their families.

This sense of belonging carries over to the company for which a person works. Indeed, the president of the company is considered a father figure and has a great responsibility toward the employees. Workers often stay with the same companies for their entire careers. People also belong to a community, and to serve the community is an honorable activity. Many Japanese have a strong sense of belonging to their nation.

There are two Japanese concepts that have to do with respect and duty. The first is *giri,* which means the responsibility of one person for another. The other is *on,* or obligation and respect for superiors, including parents, teachers, and gods. Calmness, harmony, and self-discipline are highly regarded.

# Shoguns and Samurai

When people think of Japan, they often think of the days of the shoguns and samurai. These people are special in Japanese culture. While there are no longer any shoguns or samurai in Japan, many aspects of Japanese life today have their roots in this part of the country's past.

Many of the old castles that the Japanese visit on picnics and other family outings were the homes of the daimyos who governed the provinces for the shoguns. The samurai also lived in these castles. These warriors were always ready to carry out their master's orders. At the same time, the samurai were also expected to study literature, music, and art. Because of this, they had much to do with the development of such Japanese art forms as pottery decoration and poetry writing.

*The samurai past remains a source of pride for the Japanese. At right, an actor is costumed as an ancient general. Below is a shrine dedicated to the shogun Tokugawa Ieyasu.*

The samurai lived according to a strict code, called *Bushido*, which means the "way of the warrior." The samurai themselves were called *bushi*. Bushido was based on Buddhist beliefs and on the teachings of Confucius, an ancient Chinese philosopher. The Bushido code valued honor more than life. It promoted mental and physical control and self-defense. The code influenced the development of some of Japan's traditional sports. These sports, called martial arts, include judo, kendo, and karate. Of these, the samurai practiced kendo and karate. Kendo is the art of bamboo swordmanship. Karate, which means "empty hands," is still practiced today and is popular around the world. Japanese children often take martial arts lessons in school.

Other ancient sports that are still practiced include archery and sumo wrestling. Sumo is the oldest sport in Japan. The first tournaments were held in 728, but the sport was practiced long before then. Tournaments are now presented three times a year: in January, May, and September.

Sports events, in general, are a popular form of entertainment in Japan. The most popular sport in Tokyo, as in the rest of Japan, is baseball. Children play baseball in any open space they can find. Japan's professional baseball games always attract thousands of spectators, just as baseball games do in the United States.

*Many Japanese sports are based on skills once practiced by the samurai warriors. Kendo, for example, teaches the ancient techniques of sword-fighting.*

*Archery is another skill from Japan's military past. This sport has become an important part of Buddhist instruction. Buddhists believe wisdom can be learned through physical discipline.*

Tokyo hosted the Summer Olympic Games in 1964, and the sports facilities built for those games are now open to the public. The swimming pools are especially popular. Swimming is considered very important and is taught in the public schools. In fact, most schools have an outdoor pool.

WORLD CITIES

# Places in the City

The city of Tokyo is part of a larger group of communities known as the Metropolis of Tokyo. This area, which holds about eleven million people, is made up of small cities and villages that once were separate. These smaller communities were swallowed into the city as it spread. The metropolitan area covers more than 830 square miles (2,150 sq. km). This makes Tokyo one of the largest cities in the world in area as well as in population.

The city of Tokyo itself is called the city proper. The city proper is organized into units called *ku,* a Japanese word for "ward." There are twenty-three ku in the city. Each of these is further divided into sections and numbered blocks. Because of this system, only main streets have names. This can make it difficult to find places in certain parts of the city.

Tokyo is a great city for sightseeing, for the Japanese as well as the people of other countries. The city holds many unusual buildings, gardens, temples, and shrines.

## The Imperial Palace

The gardens around the Imperial Palace, the home of Emperor Akihito in the center of Tokyo, are a popular place to visit. Japanese families come from all over the country to see this special area. The Nijubashi Bridge leads to the palace entrance. The name *Nijubashi* means "double bridge," and it refers to the bridge and its beautiful reflection shining from the water. Many people pose here for photographs.

The palace is on top of a steep hill and is surrounded by a wall that stands 50 feet (15 m) high. This wall was originally built for Edo Castle in the period of the shoguns. At that time twenty-four drawbridges, crossing three moats—or rings of water—protected the shogun's castle from invasion. Twice a year—on the second day of the new year and on the emperor's birthday—one can walk across the moats and pass through a palace gate to sign the Congratulations Register.

The Imperial Palace East Garden was opened to the public in 1968. This spot used to be the center of old Edo Castle. The new garden is larger than the previous one and includes parts of the old watchtowers, corridors, and checkpoints for the shogun's guards.

## Central Tokyo—Business, Theater, and Shopping

Central downtown Tokyo, crowded with people and automobiles, is right outside the palace grounds. Here, in the Chiyoda-ku district, are most of the government offices. These include the prime minister's office, the huge National Diet (parliament) Building, the special ministries, and the high courts. Many major banks also are located in this district.

JNTO

*Puppet theater, or bunraku, dates back to the 1600s. Some of Japan's greatest playwrights have written for the puppet shows.*

Several theaters, including the National Theater, are in this area too. Here you can see *bunraku*—Japanese puppet theater. Marionettes guided by a complicated system of strings act out bunraku, along with much larger puppets carried by actors dressed in black. Bunraku was introduced to Japan from China. Today, however, it is much more popular in Japan than it is in China.

The National Theater also offers traditional Japanese theater, or *kabuki*. The word *kabuki* means "song and dance." In this form of theater, actors in magnificent costumes perform plays with much emotion, with men taking both male and female roles. Many times the actors change the story and make up new lines as they go along. The performances can last for hours, and people in the audience come and go as they wish. Kabuki also came to Japan from China.

*Japanese class separations produced two distinct styles of drama. The colorful kabuki, performed in theaters such as that above, was popular with the merchants and shopkeepers. The more formal noh drama was preferred by the emperor and nobles (right).*

In contrast to the lively kabuki, the *noh* drama is quiet and serious. These dramas were first performed at the Kyoto court in the fifteenth century, and the music, language, and costumes date from that time. The stage is bare, except for such symbols as a branch of cherry blossoms to represent a temple garden. The dance movements of the actors also are symbolic. In the traditonal theater and dance productions, the actors wear white

rice powder on their faces, which gives them an unusual appearance.

After being entertained at the National Theater, you might go to the Ginza district in nearby Chuo-ku. This area is Tokyo's most famous shopping district. Exclusive shops and huge stores line the streets, and at night, the area is bright with colored lights. Many stores have an amusement park on the roof where children can play while their parents shop. The area is closed to automobiles on Sundays, the busiest shopping day of the

*The Ginza was the first area of Tokyo to adopt Western customs. The Japanese call such customs* haikara, *meaning "high collar."*

Harold Pfeiffer

*Fish are packed into boxes for sale to wholesalers at the Tsukiji fish market.*

## To the North—Temples, Museums, and Parks

In a district north of central Tokyo, you will find Gokokuji Temple, one of the largest Buddhist temples in Tokyo. Nearby is Korakuen Garden, an especially beautiful park. Built in 1626, it is the city's oldest park.

Farther north is Tokyo's Paper Museum, the only one of its kind in the world. In Japan, paper is considered a form of art, and this museum displays the equipment used in making paper by hand. Of course, there are displays showing many kinds of paper decorated with wonderful designs.

Returning to the central Tokyo districts, a visitor might stop at Ueno Park, one of the city's most popular attractions. This area was once part of a daimyo's home. There are paths to walk on throughout the park and a pond with boats for rent. It is the largest park in Tokyo and includes a zoo, an aquarium, and many museums, shrines, and temples.

The most notable shrine in Ueno Park is the Toshogu Shrine, established in 1627. A path lined with stone and bronze lanterns leads up to it. Some of Tokyo's most famous museums are also in this park, including the Metropolitan Fine Art Gallery, the National Museum (which displays more than 100,000 pieces of Japanese,

week for many people who spend the other six days on their jobs. Tokugawa Ieyasu established a silver mint here, and during the Edo period, the area was the commercial center of the city. Today, it also is a famous theater district.

*Asakusa,* where vendors sell goods beneath long rows of canopies, is another popular shopping center in Tokyo. *Shibaura* is the best-known market for meat, and at *Tsukiji,* the huge fish market, more than 2,500 tons of fish are sold each day. At Shibaura and Tsukiji, the buyers are mostly wholesalers and restaurant and market owners.

*The canopied shops of the Asakusa district are visible through the gate of the Asakusa Kannon Temple.*

Chinese, and Indian art), the National Science Museum, and the National Museum of Western Art.

Kannon Temple, in the nearby Asakusa district, is surrounded by many little streets without names. These streets are lined with smaller temples. The temple in Asakusa is dedicated to Kannon, the Buddhist goddess of compassion. The buildings have been destroyed several times but have always been restored.

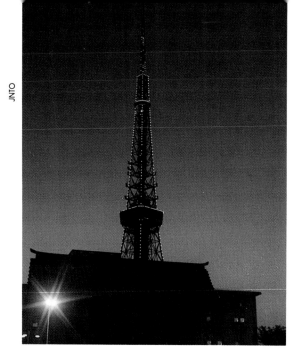
JNTO

*The Tokyo Tower (above) was modeled after the Eiffel Tower in Paris. On its fifth floor, the tower houses the studios of T.V. Tokyo. The Meiji Shrine (right), built in 1920, honors the Emperor Meiji.*

## To the South—Tokyo Tower and More Temples

In a district south of central Tokyo, it is easy to see Tokyo Tower. The tower is the tallest structure in Tokyo and is modeled after the Eiffel Tower in Paris. The tower was erected in 1958 as a symbol of Tokyo's postwar rebuilding. You can climb or take an elevator to the top for a great view. Several television and radio stations use the tower for transmitting signals, and restaurants and cafes are found nearby.

A little farther south is the Taka-nawa area of Tokyo where people visit the Sengakuji Temple. Forty-seven famous samurai are buried here. They became *ronins*—which are samurai warriors without a master—when their master was tricked into committing a crime. Because of the crime, he was required to commit *seppuku,* or ritual suicide. The forty-seven ronins finally avenged their master's death by killing the person who had tricked him. Following this, according to the samu-

rai code, they also committed seppu-ku. They are all buried in this temple cemetery.

Traveling west from here brings one to the Meiji Shrine. This shrine is one of Tokyo's most popular places of Shinto worship. It was built in 1920 and dedicated to the Emperor Meiji, who brought Japan into the modern era. The shrine's main torii, or gate, is especially impressive, for it is the tallest wooden gate in Tokyo. Visiting Shintoists pour water over their hands and cleanse their mouths at the fountain near the shrine's entrance. They also remove their hats and coats before entering. The most important festivals celebrated at this shrine include the birthday of Emperor Meiji, a festival of spring, and New Year's Day.

# A Year of Festivals

No matter what time of year it is, there is likely to be a celebration of some kind in Tokyo. The New Year's festival takes place the first week in January. In February is *Setsubun,* the bean-throwing festival. According to the old lunar calendar, this was the last day of the year. Beans are thrown to scare off the devil.

March, April, and May are busy festival months. The *Hina Matsura* is held in March. This is the dolls' festival. It is held in the home where dolls representing the emperor, empress, and members of their court are arranged on special shelves. Another festival, Girl's Day, is held with the dolls' festival. It is celebrated on the third day of the third month. April is the time for the Cherry Blossom Fes-

*The Sanja Festival, celebrated on the weekend closest to May 17, is one of Tokyo's major festivals.*

tival, an especially beautiful time of the year. Then on April 8, Japan celebrates Buddha's birthday with *Hana Matsura,* or flower festival. In Tokyo, the Sensoji Temple is a good place to visit during this festival. Finally, Boys' Day is the fifth day of the fifth month. Today, it is often called Children's Day. Proud parents fly fish-shaped banners of bright colors on this day.

During June, July, and August, there are the Summer Festivals, with many fireworks displays. The Autumn Festival is celebrated at Yasukuni Shrine. Noh dramas are presented, and there is an archery competition. In November comes *Shichi-go-san,* or Seven-five-three. All boys who are seven or five, and all girls who are seven or three, dress up in their best kimonos and visit shrines with their parents.

At the end of the year, Tokyo celebrates *Gishi Sai.* This is the festival of the forty-seven ronins, centered on the Sengakuji Temple. Also toward the year's end is Christmas. Although less than 1 percent of the Japanese people are Christians, many celebrate Christmas—without the religious part. The stores are crowded with shoppers, and displays feature Santa and his reindeer. Many of the shoppers are not buying Christmas presents, however. At the end of the year in Japan it is customary to give thank-you gifts.

During November's Shichi-go-san Festival, children of ages seven, five, and three visit Shinto shrines and pray for good fortune. It was once believed that these numbers were unlucky and that children of these ages needed special protection.

# Growth, Transportation, and Communication

Tokyo is Japan's most important commercial city. Sixty-six percent of all Japanese firms have their head-quarters in Tokyo, and most of the main offices for Japanese banks are here. Many American and European banks and businesses have branch offices in Tokyo. Two-thirds of all products brought into the country come through Tokyo, and one-third of all products sent to other countries are sent out through Tokyo.

Tokyo has become a popular place for international business conferences as well as for tourism. As a result, the hotel industry and other services have contributed much to Tokyo's economy.

In the past two decades, the stan-dard of living for the people of Tokyo and all of Japan has improved. But Tokyo also faces problems due to growth and success. Space is one of the biggest problems. Although the city seemed crowded forty years ago, Tokyo's population has continued to grow as the city has spread out to the west, north, and south.

To slow down population growth in general, the government encouraged families to have fewer children. By the late 1970s, the population was not increasing so rapidly, but a shortage of housing remains a problem in Tokyo and other crowded cities.

"New towns" have been built in surrounding districts, such as Shibuya, Ikebukuro, and Shinjuku. These are now like subcenters of Tokyo. Offices, schools, and factories have moved to these new subcenters, and small concrete homes and large apartment complexes, called *danchi*, have been built on the vacated spots. Some of Tokyo's large companies have built apartment buildings for their employees to live in. These are called *shataku*. Some low areas around Tokyo Bay have been "reclaimed," or filled in, to be used for parks and residential complexes.

New York responded to its shortage of space by building skyscrapers. In the past, this has not been the best solution for Tokyo because of earthquakes and typhoons. New building techniques to protect against damage by earthquakes now make tall buildings possible, however. The tallest building in Tokyo is the Sunshine Building, which is sixty stories high. The World Trade Center Building is forty stories, and the Shinjuku Sumitomo Building is fifty-six stories high.

Pollution is another problem associated with rapid growth. The increasing number of cars is one of the biggest causes of pollution, and smoke from the huge number of factories is another important cause. The government of Tokyo has worked to solve pollution problems. It has had some success against air pollution and against the pollution of rivers with waste materials.

Bicycles are an easy way to travel through Tokyo's crowded streets.

## Transporting People

Tokyo has a great network of railroads. Some are owned by private companies, and others are owned by the government. This network provides an efficient method to get around in Tokyo.

Tokyo Station serves as the city's center for transportation systems. The underground, or subway, has more than 100 miles (160 km) of track, and it is the most important means of transporting people within the central part of the city. Subway trains are especially crowded during rush hours. They are so crowded that some subway workers' only job is to shove passengers into the coaches so that the doors can be closed. These workers are actually called "pushers."

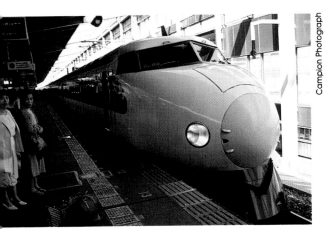

*Tokyo's traffic problems have made mass transit a necessity here (top). Now, high-speed "bullet trains" take commuters in and out of the city (bottom).*

Trains are another method of travel. The Yamanote Line of the Japanese National Railroad is a green and white train that runs above ground and circles the city. Many tourist spots are within easy walking distance of the train's numerous stations.

The famous *shinkansen,* or "bullet trains," take people to and from the city and suburbs and neighboring cities. The Japanese National Railroad operates these trains, which leave Tokyo every thirty minutes and travel at an average of 125 miles (200 km) per hour. The shinkansen is the main link to the areas north and south of the city. A highway leads to these areas, but the traffic is always heavy.

Riding in a car or a bus is the least efficient way of getting around in Tokyo and nearby areas. Traffic jams are frequent.

Transportation systems for travel beyond the city also grow increasingly busy. Tokyo's harbors and its international airport are busy with ships and planes from around the world. More than two hundred ships sail in and out of Tokyo Bay every day.

## Communications

Tokyo is the center of the communications industry for Japan. Japan is a nation of readers, and many homes receive two newspapers a day. Most of the major newspapers and more than half of all the books and magazines in Japan are published in Tokyo. Radio and television also are important means of communication, and the Japan Broadcasting Corporation has its headquarters in Tokyo.

WORLD

CITIES

# More Places In and Around Tokyo

Other districts in Tokyo include Roppongi, an international district whose name means "six trees." Many Western diplomats live here. European-style nightlife is found in cafes and nightclubs in Roppongi. It is considered an elegant place in which to live.

Daikan-vama, on the city's outskirts, is a newer residential section. It has many hillside-terrace apartments and shops.

The Harajuku district is considered the children's capital of Tokyo. All shops in the area cater to young buyers, and young people gather here for dances in the parks.

Marunouchi is the best-known business address in Tokyo. The Mitsubi-shi Company began to develop the area one hundred years ago, and most of the major companies have their headquarters here today. Its location close to Tokyo Station contributed to the area's growth and success. Once known as "Little London," Marunouchi is noted for its sacred buildings, museums, theaters, and the National Library, as well as for its business activity during the time of the shoguns, when the city was called Edo. Fish markets, craft shops, and the banking industry were all located here. Today the area holds banks, government offices, and department stores.

Tsukudamima is a district southwest of central Tokyo. This area escaped much of the damage that the city endured during World War II. More than anywhere else in Tokyo, many of the streets here look much as they did during the Edo period.

## Kamakura and Yokohama

Kamakura is 30 miles (48 km) south of central Tokyo. This city was the headquarters for Japan's first shogun in the twelfth century. It is a favorite seaside resort for the people who live in Tokyo, and it has many attractions for tourists, including more than eighty temples and shrines. One of the greatest attractions in Kamakura is the statue of the *Great Buddha.* Constructed in 1252, it weighs 100 tons and is 40 feet (12 m) tall. Today the statue belongs to Kotokuin Temple.

Hachimangu Shrine is especially worth visiting. It was established in 1063 to honor Emperor Ojim of the third century as the god of war. A building added to the shrine in 1828 is covered with colored carvings, and the ginkgo tree standing in front of the shrine is said to be more than one thousand years old.

The city of Yokohama, a busy seaport, is just 18 miles (29 km) south of Tokyo. Yokohama's harbor is deeper than Tokyo's, which means that it can handle bigger ships. Most of Japan's

Jack Com

*Above is the face of Kotokuin Temple's 100-ton statue of the* Great Buddha. *Yokohama harbor is Japan's most important port for ocean-going ships (opposite, above). Tsukudjima escaped bombing during World War II and has retained the look of pre-war Tokyo (opposite, below).*

imports and exports go through this port. Japan first opened the country at Yokohama, and in 1859, Japan allowed foreigners to settle in the city. Many still like to live here today.

*Autumn colors tint the foothills of Mount Fuji, Japan's sacred mountain. The snow-capped peak has long been a favorite subject for Japanese artists.*

Many people consider the cities of Tokyo and Yokohama one large "supercity." With a population of 20 million people in 1983, it is the largest supercity in the world. Some people think that Mexico City will be the largest supercity by the year 2025. Today its population is estimated at 18 million. By 2025, it is expected to have a population of more than 36 million. The supercity of Tokyo-Yokohama is expected to grow by less than 1 million, to perhaps 20.7 million people.

## Mount Fuji

The greatest landmark of the Tokyo area, famous the world over, is Mount Fuji. The Japanese call it *Fuji-san,* and it is their sacred mountain. It is 12,390 feet (3,776 m) high. Often the peak is covered by clouds or smog, but on clear days it presents a sight no one ever forgets. Mount Fuji is a volcanic mountain, but it is not active. It last erupted in 1707.

Every summer, more than 100,000 people climb to the peak. During the winter there is too much snow and ice on the mountain, making the routes to the top impassable. There are six mountain paths, each with many resting places. It is said that watching the sun rise from atop Fuji-san is one of the most beautiful experiences in the world.

# Tokyo—A World City

Tokyo is a city of contrasts, bringing together the old and the new. Tokyo theater groups carry on tradition with kabuki productions, bunraku puppet plays, and noh dramas, all of which are highly popular. Traditional Japanese music also is popular, and so is Western music, especially that composed by Mozart and Beethoven. Tokyo has seven orchestras, including the Japan Philharmonic and the Tokyo Symphony. Their concerts are always well attended.

In Tokyo, the National Science Museum and the National Museum of Western Art exist side by side with traditional displays found in the Paper Museum, the Silk Museum, the Japan Calligraphy Museum, the Folkcrafts Museum, the Kite Museum, and the Costume Museum. The Japanese Sword Museum is special. Here one can see displays of beautiful swords of the past and learn about both ancient and modern ways of making swords.

The people of Tokyo enjoy going to movies and watching television. They also enjoy traditional landscape painting, the tea ceremony, and haiku poetry. Baseball is popular with millions of people, just as ancient sumo wrestling is.

Tokyo is a city of small shops and open-air markets, and also a city with large department stores and tall buildings whose streets are crowded with automobiles. It is a city of traditional crafts people and one in which are

*The Shinjuku district contains more skyscrapers than any other part of Tokyo. The oldest building here dates back only to 1971.*

found industries that manufacture steel, electronics goods, automobiles, and jet airplanes. Some factories are small, with fewer than twenty workers each. Others are gigantic, with from ten thousand to twenty thousand workers each.

Automobile traffic jams are frequent in Tokyo, yet the city has a highly efficient subway and above-ground rail system, and a monorail connecting central Tokyo with Tokyo International Airport in the far southern part of the city. There, jetliners take off for and arrive from all the world's major cities.

Trade is the lifeblood of Tokyo and of all Japan, and in Tokyo nearly three thousand companies deal in trade with other countries. Raw materials such as coal and oil come to the city from abroad, and automobiles, electronic goods, and other products are shipped from the ports of Tokyo and Yokohama to countries all over the world.

Tokyo rose from the ashes of World War II to become the center of a new Japan, a modern city with many touches of the traditional, taking its place among the important cities of the world.

# Tokyo: Historical Events

**300 B.C.** Marks the earliest evidence of inhabitants in the Tokyo area.

**A.D. 400s** The leader of the Yamato tribe takes the title of *emperor*.

**710** The city of Nara becomes the first Japanese capital.

**728** The first sumo tournaments are held.

**790** The capital is moved to Kyoto.

**1192** Minamoto Yoritomo forms the first shogunate and becomes the the first shogun.

**1274** Kublai Khan sends his army on its first invasion of Japan. The army turns back in the face of stormy weather.

**1281** Kublai Khan's second invasion of Japan is defeated by a great typhoon the Japanese call *kamikaze*, a "divine wind."

**1338** The Ashikaga family achieves power.

**1400s** The small village of Edo is transformed into a military city.

**1540s** The first Catholic missionaries from Portugal arrive in Japan.

**1590** Tokugawa Ieyasu takes possession of Edo Castle.

**1603** Tokugawa Ieyasu becomes shogun.

**1626** Korakuen Park, Edo's oldest park, is completed.

**1627** The Toshogu Shrine is built.

**1636** Japan withdraws from the world to begin a period of more than two hundred years of isolation.

**1657** A great fire in Edo kills 100,000 people.

**1707** Mount Fuji erupts for the last time to date.

**1853** The period of isolation ends as Japan becomes open to the world once again.

**1868** The power of the emperor is restored. The capital is moved to Edo, which is renamed Tokyo.

**1876** The samurai lose their last symbol of power when they are forbidden to wear their swords.

**1889** Japan's first constitution is written and goes into effect.

**1920** The Meiji Shrine is completed.

**1923** A great earthquake destroys much of Tokyo, killing sixty thousand people.

**1930s** Japan invades China.

**1941** The Japanese attack Pearl Harbor.

**1945** The United States drops atomic bombs on Hiroshima and Nagasaki. The Japanese surrender, ending World War II.

**1952** The American occupation forces leave Japan.

**1958** Tokyo Tower is completed.

**1964** Tokyo hosts the Summer Olympic Games.

**1968** The Imperial Palace East Garden is opened to the public.

**1989** Crown Prince Akihito becomes emperor upon the death of Hirohito.

# Downtown Tokyo

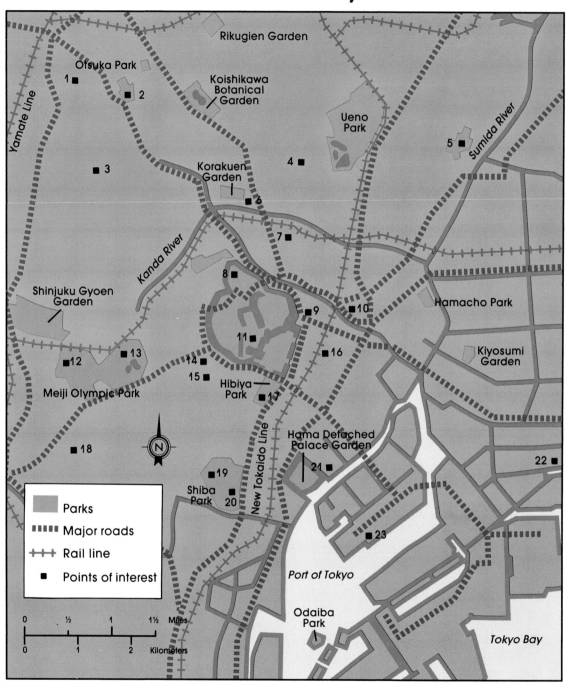

Rikugien Garden

Otsuka Park

1 ■

2 ■

Koishikawa
Botanical
Garden

Ueno
Park

5 ■

Sumida River

Yamate Line

3 ■

4 ■

Korakuen
Garden

6 ■

Kanda River

7 ■

8 ■

Shinjuku Gyoen
Garden

9 ■

10 ■

Hamacho Park

11 ■

16 ■

Kiyosumi
Garden

12 ■

13 ■

14 ■

15 ■

Hibiya
Park

17 ■

Meiji Olympic Park

N

18 ■

New Tokaido Line

Hama Detached
Palace Garden

21 ■

22 ■

19 ■

Shiba
Park

20 ■

23 ■

Parks

Major roads

Rail line

Points of interest

Port of Tokyo

Odaiba
Park

Tokyo Bay

0     ½     1     1½   Miles

0     1     2   Kilometers

# Map Key

## Points of Interest

1 Kishibojin Temple
2 Gokokuji Temple
3 Waseda University
4 Tokyo University
5 Kannon Temple
6 Korakuen Stadium
7 Meiji University
8 National Museum of Modern Art
9 Trade Center
10 Bank of Japan
11 Imperial Palace
12 National Stadium
13 Akasaka Detached Palace
14 National Diet Library
15 National Diet Building
16 Tokyo Station
17 Hibiya Library
18 Nezu Art Museum
19 Tokyo Tower
20 Zojoji Temple
21 Central Wholesale Market
22 Tokyo Heliport
23 Harumi International Trade Center

# Tokyo Almanac

**Location:** Latitude—35.4° north. Longitude—139.4° east.

**Climate:** Subtropical. Average January temperature—40°F (4°C). Average July temperature —79°F (26°C). Average annual precipitation—61 inches (155 cm).

**Land Area:** 229 sq. miles (593 sq. km).

**Population:** City proper—8,386,000 people (1986 census). Metropolitan area—11,635,000. World ranking—5. Population density—29,874 persons/sq. mile.

**Major Airports:** Narita (The New Tokyo International Airport) and Haneda (Tokyo International Airport) handle 7,390,700 passengers a year.

**Colleges/Universities:** 190 colleges, universities, and other institutions of higher learning, including University of Tokyo, Tokyo Metropolitan University, Keio University, Waseda University, Yokohama City University, and Nihon University.

**Medical Facilities:** Hospital beds—66,150. Doctors—36,100. Nurses—22,300.

**Media:** Newspapers—main newspapers are *Asahi* and *Mainichi*. Television—Japan Broadcasting Corporation is the main network with 10+ commercial stations.

**Major Buildings:** World Trade Center—40 stories, 499 feet (152 m). Mitsui Masumigaseki—44 stories, approximately 482 feet (147 m). Keio Plaza Hotel—51 stories, approximately 558 feet (170 m). Sunshine Building—60 stories, approximately 660 feet (201 m). Tokyo Tower—1,100 feet (335 m).

**Ports:** The ports of Tokyo, Yokohama, Kawasaki, and Chiba handle 228,552,000 tons/year total.

**Transportation:** Commuter trains handle 10 million passengers/day.

**Interesting Fact:** The city of Tokyo has a Disneyland on Tokyo Bay.

# Index